T0161052

TAPESTRY

POEMS OF
LIFE AND LOVE

KATHRYN CAROLE ELLISON

Published by Lady Bug Books, an imprint of Brisance Books Group.
Lady Bug Press and the distinctive ladybug logo are registered trademarks of
Lady Bug Books, LLC.

Lady Bug Books
400 112th Avenue N.E.
Suite 230
Bellevue, WA 98004
www.giftsoflove.com

For information about custom editions, special sales and permissions, please contact
Brisance Books Group at specialsales@brisancebooksgroup.com

Manufactured in the United States of America
ISBN: 978-1-944194-59-8

First Edition: October 2019

A NOTE FROM THE AUTHOR

The poems in this book were written over many years as gifts to my children. I began writing them in the 1970s, when they were reaching the age of reason. And, as I found myself in the position of becoming a single parent, I wanted to do something special to share with them—something that would become a tradition, a ritual they could count on.

And so the Advent Poems began—one day, decades ago—with a poem 'gifted' to them each day during the Advent period leading up to Christmas, December 1 to December 24. Forty some years later... my children still look forward each year to the poems that started a family tradition, that new generations have come to cherish.

It is my sincere hope that you will embrace and enjoy them, and share them with those you love.

Children of the Light was among the early poems I wrote, and is included in each of the *Poems of Life and Love* books in The Ellison Collection: *Heartstrings, Celebrations, Inspirations, Sanctuary, Awakenings, Sojourns, Milestones, Tapestry* and *Gratitude.* After writing many hundreds of poems, it is still my favorite. The words came from my heart... and my soul... and flowed so effortlessly that it was written in a single sitting. All I needed to do was capture the words on paper.

Light, to me, represented all that was good and pure and right with the world, and I believed then—as I do today—that those elements live in my children, and perhaps in all of us. We need only to dare.

– KCE

DEDICATION

To my parents: Herb and Bernice Haas

Mom, you were the poet who went before me...
unpublished, but appreciated nonetheless.

And Dad, you always believed in me,
no matter what direction my life took.
Thank you for your faith in me,
and for your unconditional love.

TABLE OF CONTENTS

LIFE'S JOYS

LIFE'S LESSONS

LIFE'S GIFTS

LIFE'S JOYS

TAPESTRY

In the tapestry of life, we're all connected.
Each one of us is a gift to the other.
We help each other to be who we are.
We make a perfect picture together.

Yes, the connections we make throughout the day
Weave our tapestry of life. They're intertwined.
Individually, we're all only fragile threads,
But what a tapestry we make when combined!

Life is not a series of coincidences,
But a tapestry of events as we live our days.
The events culminate into an exquisite plan.
Our tapestry defines us in so many ways.

Your collection of experiences, every part of your life,
Are the threads of your tapestry, I wish to impart.
Weave your life experiences into a beautiful picture.
Make the story of your life into art.

CONNECTEDNESS

Each action that we do or think or say
Imprints upon those met along the way.
We trace our paths through life and find that we
Are linked with all that's in our galaxy.

We're part of what's gone on in years before,
Connected back beyond the days of yore.
We're part of what is happening right now,
And must be mindful of what we endow.

For action that we take while we're alive
Determines how our galaxy will survive.
It's may be strange to think in terms like these,
But for today, be loving, will you please?

CHILDREN OF THE LIGHT

There are those souls who bring the light,
Who spill it out for all to share.
And with a joy that does excite,
They show the world that they do care.
It is so very bright.

In this sharing, love does pervade
Into their lives and cycles round;
And as this light is outward played
The love is also inward bound.
It is an awesome trade.

You are a soul whose light is shared.
It comes from deep within your heart.
It's best because it is not spared,
Because it's total, not just part.
And I am glad you've dared.

IF LAUGHTER WERE FOOD

If laughter were food I'd want three meals
Of health-giving chuckles each day;
And the flavor of my laughter would be
At no one's expense or dismay.

I'd find the choicest tidbits of mirth
About a humorous situation,
And take big bites till there were no more,
And belch only exaltation.

And then I'd turn that humor within,
And stop being quite so serious.
I'd laugh at myself and all my foibles
And dance until quite delirious!!!

Laughter is freedom—it's good for the soul,
And good for the body, as well.
So, laugh at your jokes with all your being;
Your joy will weave quite a spell!

CHANGE

There's not a tomb big enough to hold all the bones
Of the parts of ourselves that died along the way,
As changes were necessary for our very survival...
To live our lives; to face another day.

All changes have a melancholy, even those we desire,
According to Anatole France, a French novelist.
What is left behind is a part of ourselves,
But we must die to one life before another can exist.

With every new stage of life there are chances
To grieve as well as to celebrate.
We are constantly passing from one state to another,
And we're sent guides and mentors to light our way.

André Gide, another French novelist,
Said this about change (and more):
"Man cannot discover new oceans
{Without} courage to lose sight of the shore."

Your life does not get better by chance.
Your path is not prearranged.
Even if you stumble, you're still moving forward.
Your life gets better by change.

Nobody can go back and make a new beginning;
It's water under the bridge, as they say.
But anyone can make a new ending
By starting on the path today.

TODAY

It is a moment of light on all sides surrounded
By mystery... by darkness and oblivion.
There has never been another just like it
In your life or in the entire history,
And you can bet there will never be
Another like it ever again.
It's the point from which all tomorrows go
Until the hour of your death.
If you were aware how precious it is
You would hardly be able to live through it.
And, unless you are aware of how precious it is
You're hardly living at all.
The point is to see it for what it is
'Cause it will be gone before you know it.
If you waste it now it's your life you're wasting,
And your life is here right now.
If you look the other way awaiting a moment
It probably will pass you by.
All other days have either disappeared
Into darkness and oblivion,
Or haven't yet emerged for you;
Today is the only day there is.

SELF-HELP

Self-Help can be
Compared, you see,
To the likes of pumping iron.
Except it's space
Is in another place...
A less physical environ.

Manipulating weights
In pounds of eights
Builds physical strength in you.
And manipulating thoughts,
Getting rid of the 'nots,'
Builds mentally a new point of view.

BEAUTY

Beauty is to the spirit
What food is to the flesh.
You glimpse it in a face
Yet it's behind the skin.
It echoes in a song
And is seldom the melody.
Like wind moves the leaves,
Beauty invisibly transforms
Moods and aspects and sentiments.

Beauty fills your spirit
And sends your soul to soaring,
Visiting places of your dreams
That consciousness only glimpses.
When you believe you have reached
The limits that you have set
And you can contain no more,
Prepare yourself, my friends...
Your limits are self-imposed.

Experiencing leaves you aching,
After it is gone, with longing.
You long for more of the same
And you long for whatever it is
That resides down deep within
And far beyond the boundaries
Of both beauty (the beheld)
And yourself (the beholder),
That makes it beautiful.

ADVENTURE

It's said that your life truly begins
At the end of your safe place, your comfort zone.
To escape the ordinary, to feel truly free...
Adventure is the answer. Go into the unknown.

Seeking adventures that open your mind
Requires curiosity (that's your need to learn).
The curious will always have their minds filled
With stories to share upon their return.

Jobs fill your pocket; adventures fill your soul.
Adventures will lead you to where you belong.
The best view usually comes after the hardest climb.
Escape the ordinary... you can't go wrong.

Oprah, in her wisdom, said, "The biggest adventure
You can take is to live the life of your dreams."
You've nothing to lose, and the world to experience;
Plan now and make adventure a part of your schemes.

Have stories to tell, not stuff to show.
Getting lost might lead you to an amazing find!
If it scares you, it might be a good thing to try.
The possibilities are endless. Open your mind!

ACHIEVEMENTS

Life is not about finding yourself;
It's about creating yourself, as you go.
Your job is to figure out just who you want to be,
Then to be that; with a large amount of gusto!

The best achievements you'll have in your life
Come from doing things you think you cannot do;
Then believing you can do it... with great expectations.
You'll see it happen, you will, right in front of you.

Never underestimate your own strength and courage.
Great love and great achievements involve taking chances.
You were born with a purpose and you are blessed
With the power to shine in your performances.

Winners compare their own achievements
With their own goals they have pushed toward reaching;
While losers compare their achievements with those
Of other people. (There's wisdom here in this teaching.)

The world of achievement has always belonged
To the optimists who pursue their own destiny.
It's not left to chance; it's a matter of choice.
With high expectation, high achievement is guaranteed.

IT'S IN YOU

Somewhere in my reading I ran across
A few words on the subject of "doing."
Seems that one is born with a natural leaning
For the direction they should be pursuing.

Well, at first, to me, it seemed quite off-putting,
By closing the door to all who would apply.
It seemed to say, "Don't bother to knock,
Because you would fail if you try."

On further readings I found myself
In agreement with the words.
I realized the essence in those two little lines,
So listen, this needs to be heard.

If you want to attain a certain thing
You must have it in you to achieve!
Since you want to attain it, you already are
Such a person, so do not grieve.

Just know that whatever you decide to do,
It's in you to make it a success.
Take the steps to complete the tasks at hand,
And you'll do it without great stress.

TRAVEL

John Steinbeck wrote that "People don't take trips,
{But that} trips take people," and it seems to be true.
You go, expecting the trip to be a certain way,
And most times it changes your entire point of view.

"A mind that is stretched by a new experience
Can never go back to its old dimensions."
So said Oliver Wendell Holmes, a legal scholar,
When talking about travel. It can change perceptions.

Experiencing the world as we were taught
Is no longer a limiting element.
Travel insists that we see for ourselves;
And once we travel, we are no longer content
To hold onto old concepts of how the world is,
Or how people of other countries are so different.
People everywhere all cry and laugh and eat,
And worry and die—all a common ingredient.

I keep traveling clothes ready, and am open to learning.
It's my goal to be a perpetual tourist.
And, as Susan Sontag was quoted as saying:
"I haven't been everywhere, but it's on my list!"

BE HOSPITABLE

Hospitality is more than just throwing a fine party
Or cooking a meal that surpasses any other.
It means that we take people into our space...
It means that we reach out and invite another
To share our lives, our minds, and our hearts,
And let them know it is not any bother.

Hospitality is the way we come out of ourselves
By taking an interest in how others abide.
It is the first step toward the breaking down
Of barriers between people which often divide.
Hospitality turns a prejudiced world around...
One heart at a time... the love is magnified.

LIFE'S LESSONS

MEND THE WORLD

When strife occurs between nations—
Between neighbors or loved ones, as well,
An unease is felt by everyone,
It's shadows to foretell.
Pain and misery will follow
Until you can put it to rest.
There's a way to reduce the tension;
This might describe it best:

We are a part of the great woven texture
Of our world and the universe unending.
When fabric has suffered a break
The metaphor for healing is mending.
When a couple in their mud house in Africa
Maintain just and joyful relations,
The world is a little bit better place,
And they deserve our congratulations.

As members of the world community
We must run our own checks and balances,
Then make repairs to the tear in the web
And enhance, with love, our alliances.
Review your actions the past twenty-four hours;
Imagine your ability to refashion.
Mend your world one correction at a time,
Then live your life with passion.

THE GRAND ESSENTIALS

In order to achieve the best in life
(Most would say that is true happiness)
One may go through the exercise of strife
And more than just a little bit of stress
To ultimately find the sweet success.
The grand essentials for the deepest joys
Are certainly more than just a few toys.

Instead, they count in three, the first of which
Is *having something that you like to do.*
To have a feeling that you've found your niche
Is like that of your foot in the right shoe.
Your work is such that it is ever new,
It gives a reason to get up each morn.
You know there's a purpose for your being born.

The second need, fulfilled, brings so much more.
It fits just like a hand fits in a glove.
It surely makes your heart and spirit soar,
And it is *someone (or something) to love*.
You feel as if you're guided from above.
Something to love expands your point of view;
You're apt to get perceptions that are new.

The third and final element, they say,
For happiness in life takes a real shift.
It touches in a supernatural way—
To have it is to have a wondrous gift.
Without it, you are clearly cast adrift.
It is *something to hope for* in your being;
It affords a whole new way of seeing.

HEART AS FILTER

Choose to see the world through your heart,
Or through the eyes of reason?
It's a perennial question that's always at hand;
It's present in every season.

To fall into the mode of seeing the world
Through one's intellect is a cinch.
We interpret and judge, analyze and ponder
Each other's behavior to the inch.

Judgment of others blocks the ability to love
In an unconditional style.
The intellect gets in the way of the truth.
(Bear with me for awhile.)

Each little human trait or foible
Observed in your fellow man
Can be intellectually reason enough
To throw your friendship in the ash can.

Intellect does not understand the experience
Of love as YOU want to know it.
So, use your heart as a filter for seeing
The world... and never outgrow it.

PROACTIVITY

The difference between a successful person
And others is not a lack of strength...
Nor is it a lack of research and knowledge.
Goodness knows that scholars go to great lengths!

No, the difference lies mainly in the spine of the person,
And how much enterprise he is able to use...
How well he stays focused in pursuing his dream.
His will brings success to the path he chooses.

Proactive people don't wait at the shore
For their ship to come in to port.
They swim out to meet it... they greet it with a smile.
(Swimming is a marvelous sport!)

A relatively good plan that you act on today
Can be better than a perfect one tomorrow.
Success does not come to those who wait.
It's there for the taking... the gap is narrow.

Proactive people do something every day
That will inch them closer to a better future.
If opportunity doesn't knock, they build a door.
(By now, you're beginning to get the picture.)

THE BLAME GAME

Anger is a passion that is all-consuming;
It poisons your thoughts and your senses.
Right actions get tabled and madness prevails.
You overreact to any outside offenses.

Preoccupation with this burning rage
Tamps down your growth, that's for sure.
It makes you second-rate people, you know,
And incredibly immature.

The contributions you were meant to make
As citizens of the universe
Get sidelined by this opposing host—
This anger makes matters worse.

Soon blame starts creeping through the cracks:
("It's surely their fault, not mine.")
And others' faults become your focus.
The whole thing's quite asinine.

You know that blaming is a dead-end road,
And surely not the best tool for growth.
If you let go of blaming and anger,
Success is guaranteed to you both.

SENSE FUTURE GENERATIONS

Imagine you are surrounded by
Your descendants—your future generations.
What knowledge do they need that you have now
To pass on for their situations?

Your life pulses back to the beginnings of the Earth—
Your heart beats in time to those who come after.
With your imagination you can sense their needs.
They are breathing your rhythm in the hereafter.

Do you feel them hovering like a cloud of observers
To learn from you? They're your clan.
They and their claim to life is real,
So teach them what you can.

COMMITMENT TO YOURSELF

Until one is committed there's the chance to draw back,
And hesitancy and weakness take their toll.
What seemed like shining diamonds yesterday
Is today just a bucket of coal.

But remember there is one elementary truth,
The ignorance of which kills off dreams.
When you commit with all your might,
Then Providence moves mountains, it seems.

When you commit with all your might
Things fall into place one by one.
What seemed impossible to overcome by events,
An assurance to succeed is won.

Goethe stated: "Whatever you can do,
Or dream you can, begin it..."
Continuing on with, "Boldness has genius,"
With power and magic in it.

APPEARANCE VS. REALITY

It would be a different world
If you understood the source of your reality.
Events are seen through your own perceptions:
Things happen; You react; Your impression is a 'finality.'
You see by what you're conditioned to see.
Your input is placed into various categories.
Categories are handed down by family and friends,
Or by our culture: They are transitory!

Your minds are limited by what you attend to,
And you choose the message with which you mostly agree.
No two people have identical views.
Your personal history determines what you hear and see.

How you see the world is your responsibility.
As adults you can shed any earlier influence.
Losing stereotyping and other peoples' biases,
And thinking clearly for yourselves just makes sense.

When events occur, avoid hasty conclusions.
Take more time: be patient. See the whole thing.
Be willing and available to hear another view.
To your old opinion "tapes," no longer cling.

WORDS AND MUSIC

Listen closely, it's there for you to hear.
Can you hear the music playing?
Your thoughts which emanate from inside your mind
Make the music you are saying.

The rhythm of words is music to the ears,
Even if the tune is hard to find.
'Tune' is the meaning, or what you 'hear.'
The music is there to challenge the mind.

In poetry, the shape and sound of the words
Are as wonderful as their meaning to you.
The rhythmic flow of sound is music.
It's all the same... a fact to pursue.

Poetry is about flow and rhythm and meaning,
And is expressed in music and speech.
The flowing of words or the sounds from the instruments
Are all part of the same thing, I would teach.

YOUR FUTURE

Are you so busy living your lives day to day
That you don't ask yourself what is your pathway?
˙What kind of person do I want to be?˙
Is one question to put to yourself, you see.

And, ˙What are my personal ideals as I live?˙
˙Whom do I admire?˙ ˙What is my objective?˙
Write down in a notebook your list of traits,
Then practice them daily; do not vacillate.

It's time to stop being vague about your goal.
Without attention to it, you're only playing a role.
Decide, then practice, who you want to be,
And be that person most certainly.

EITHER... OR

Either you are sunshine
Or rain in another's life.
You can go through life with joy
Or live it out in strife.

Words you speak can be cancer,
Or the cure, it seems to me.
They can repress a soul from growing
Or refresh, like a breeze from the sea.

We are all of us totally capable
Of living on a positive plane;
Or a negative one—our choice:
To bring joy or just complain.

The choice is yours to make:
How do you wish to live?
Either giving and receiving grief...
Or being actively positive?

LABELS

Labels, as such, are generalizations,
Painting each person with a broad brush.
They're often imposed from the outside world,
And you can assume them in your rush
To fulfill a preconceived image that
You've held or bought into in order to fit
What you thought was required in order to belong;
When in reality you were a hypocrite.

Stay true to yourself; believe in your good.
You've so much to offer the world at large.
Write all of your own true outlines for living!
Believe in yourself! You are in charge!

Remember this lesson and mark it well.
By living a "label" that doesn't fit,
You've molded a life for yourself that is false.
So remove that label—and get on with it.

RESPECT

A definition of friendship is built on two things:
These two are respect and trust.
Without the two in mutual accord
The friendship will turn to rust.

Respect implies imagination, the ability to see
One another across your differences.
It's a two-way street, this thing known as respect.
To get it, you must give it. (Take down fences.)

It is one of the greatest expressions of love.
Love is honesty; a mutual respect for one another.
Nothing of real worth can ever be bought.
Love and respect are earned. (Not the other!)

Loss of self-respect is the world's greatest loss.
This truth, within you, must inhabit.
Do not expect others to treat you with respect
When, to yourself, you don't even show it!

Respect your efforts, respect yourself.
Self-respect eventually leads to great strength.
Respect for yourself will guide your morals;
Respect for others guides your manners, at length.

CENTERING

The key to centering is a long, deep breath.
Let emotions go and let your mind be free.
Stay centered by accepting whatever you are doing.
Be calm, clear and thoughtful, shut down the "committee."

At the center of your being you have your answer.
You know who you are and who you want to be.
You know the present moment is the only one to control...
Your actions, not the results. You won't disagree.

Peace comes from within; do not seek it from without.
Your life is shaped by your mind, you become what you think.
With your thoughts you make your world, so be in the present.
Your choices will be healthy, your life will stay in synch.

LIFE'S GIFTS

MOSAIC

None of us is alone in this world.
We are each a vital piece of the whole...
The whole of humanity, the entire population...
That's nation by nation, each and every soul.

We're a Mosaic, not of groups, but of individuals.
We each carry a host of cultural influences.
The Mosaic is held together by the common pursuit of happiness,
The most powerful mortar, its strength is immense.

We are not a melting-pot, but a beautiful Mosaic
Of different backgrounds, beliefs, and different colors of skin.
We're all immigrants who bring the beauty of our origins
To be anchored in a new culture where we are all kin.

LOVE YOUR SPACE

A mundane building can be transformed
Through the spirit with which it is well warmed.
Make sure your own spirit is well-formed.

A bouquet of flowers on your table;
A well-scrubbed doorstep, if you're able,
Or the smell of fresh bread beneath your gable.

It's significant that you have done your best,
And not the least—and not on request,
And done with love, not as a test.

Write a love letter to where you live.
Praise its traits that are positive.
List specifics in the praises you give.

CURIOSITY

We are all explorers, all seeking something
Beyond our reach... perhaps something we have lost.
It is seldom we will find it; attainment is secondary,
For the greater happiness is in the quest.

Our work reveals what is still not understood.
The questions we have continue to be.
Consider the iceberg as a parallel image.
It is amazing how much our minds don't yet see.

Eleanor Roosevelt prized curiosity above all.
She proclaimed it a most useful gift
For a child at birth to receive this passion,
To live a life that for itself could only uplift.

Albert Einstein (The Curious) once said about the subject
That curiosity has its own reason, or occupation
To exist in our lives; and furthermore he said,
"It's a miracle that curiosity survives formal education."

Plutarch (before Christ), when speaking of the mind,
Said it was not a vessel to be filled;
But a fire to be kindled (throughout one's lifetime).
Curiosity brings much learning to be distilled.

"The love of knowledge is a kind of madness."
(So says C. S. Lewis... his take on the subject.)
"Sometimes questions are more important than the answer."
(Nancy Willard was being most circumspect.)

So seize the moment of your excited curiosity
On any subject to solve any doubts you might carry!
If you let the moment pass, it may be gone forever!
And ignorance will be more than temporary!

LAUGHTER'S VICTORY

Laughter's magic will overcome
The mood that settles round the room
When struggle empowers. You are numb,
And then laughter, like a broom,
Whisks it away and lifts the gloom.

There's mystery about the way
That laughter lifts the gloomy vein.
Contagion is what saves the day.
It weaves throughout, it's skein on skein.
Before you know there is no pain.

If you fall victim to the view
That you must struggle all alone,
Remember that the choice you drew
Is yours, although the way's been shown
To win with laughter. Love is known.

The magic is yours to use and share;
It flows so freely through the sky.
To laugh in the face of struggle is rare,
But worth the effort. It's good to try,
And laughter will replace your sigh.

ABOUT TRUE FRIENDS

About true friends: there are lots of them...
Some you do not know today.
As you go along your life's path in joy,
They'll show up, share a smile, and stay.

They'll enrich your lives as you do theirs,
'Cause you'll love them and let them go
To pursue their goals and find their path;
And they'll always be a part of your "show."

True friends leave a legacy; a part of them
Is left behind in your heart.
And when reunion occurs and paths cross again
It's as if you were never apart.

CENTERED AND GROUNDED

People who are centered and grounded are able
To work with those erratic and unstable.
They can bring a mix of folks to agreement...
Folks whose aims begin in great dissent...
To meet and share ideas round the table.

Being centered is being able to recover
One's balance in the midst of action; moreover
A centered person is not subject to whims
Or sudden excitements, leaving others out on limbs.
Being centered, a person is open to discover.

Being grounded just means being down to earth,
But not experiencing life without mirth.
It's knowing where one stands on any subject;
And knowing what one stands for with respect
To right and wrong, attaining one's self worth.

AN INSPIRATIONAL LIFE

Albert Einstein had a very bright mind.
He was remembered for his formula, E=mc squared.
But he is also known for some very wise words:
Regarding inspiration, these words he shared:
"There are two ways to live your life," said he,
"One is as though nothing is a miracle;
The other is as though everything is."
Was Einstein some kind of oracle?

In doing, don't ask what the world needs.
Ask only what makes you come alive.
Then go do it, and make the world a better place.
It needs more people who thrive!

And don't worry about failures; no, not a bit.
Sure, you might end up having some of them.
Worry instead about the chances you'd miss;
When you don't even try, it's a problem.

You alone must build your very own dreams
For a life of happiness, you know;
Or someone will hire you to build some for them,
Leaving you to live a life of sorrow.

WHO ARE YOU?

Ever wonder about who you really are
Beyond the bond of roles you choose to take—
The self that is authentic at your core,
The self you never ever should forsake?

You're not defined by roles, as we discussed,
Or by your job or function, day by day.
As there are many things of which you are not,
To find your "self" you must not go astray.

You really are a wonderful composite
Of every gift that is unique to you—
Your charm, your skills, abilities and interests;
Your talents, insights—yes, and wisdom, too.

If you should find that in your daily living
You are not true to your authentic core,
An ever-present feeling will surround you
Of lack, and then you think there should be more.

You'll think you should be doing something different;
You'll feel an incompleteness in your soul.
You'll be swayed by others' thoughts and by their actions;
You'll feel passed by, and somehow less than whole.

Your attitude, along with your soul searching,
Will make a difference in your life. Just say,
"The quality that I have as a unique being
Gives me the right to be here every day."

It matters that the challenge be yours only
As you rewrite and prove your own reality.
And then you're able to live your life with freedom
To be just who you are with new vitality.

GENDER QUEST

Males are strong and daring and aggressive;
Females are sensitive and gentle.
At least, that's the way it used to be;
The whole thing was elemental.

Although artists and actors and maybe some priests
Were allowed to behave out of norm,
Everyone knew they were odd to begin with,
So didn't insist they conform.

Fortunately the stereotypes began to break down
In the sixties with the HAIR revolution,
Liberating the males and the females alike
For a more meaningful contribution.

Opposing war and violence or nuclear power
Was not a slap in the face of manhood,
And women who worked and brought home the bacon
Had a better chance of being understood.

There's still confusion about the new liberations;
More roles are available for the taking.
Ay, the rub is defining for one's own path
What is worthy of undertaking.

Father and husband, brother and son...
These roles aren't 'in charge' as before.
Mother and wife, sister and daughter...
There's ever more room to explore.

The roles of lover and that of friend
Take on new meaning, with insight...
Judgment of others is replaced by acceptance
And everything's seen in new light.

WE ALL NEED EACH OTHER

Like tiles in a mosaic our lives are joined,
Creating patterns that complete the whole.
We're in each other's world by grand design
To love and help each other toward the goal.

We're necessary, one and all, believe me;
So lock arms and move forward all together
With those who need you and your special talents.
You need them, too, to brave all kinds of weather.

We use each other to reduce the burden
By sharing what is weighing down our soul.
Conversely, sharing joys can double pleasures,
Allowing hearts the room to freely gambol.

A CLOSING THOUGHT

POETRY

It's the revelation
Of a sensation
That the poet
(Wouldn't you know it)
Believes to be
Felt only interiorly
And personal to
The writer who
… **writes it.**

It's the interpretation
Of a sensation
That was fueled by
A poet's sigh
And believed to be
Shared mutually
And personal to
The lucky one who
… **reads it.**

About the author

Kathryn Carole Ellison is a former newspaper columnist
and journalist and, of course, a poet.

She lives near her children and stepchildren and their families in the
Pacific Northwest, and spends winters in the sunshine of Arizona.

You might find her on the golf course with friends, river rafting, traveling
the world, writing poems... or enjoying the Opera and the Symphony.

Late bloomer

Our culture honors youth with all
It's unbridled effervescence.
We older ones sit back and nod
As if in acquiescence.

And when our confidence really gels
In early convalescence...
'We can't be getting old!' we cry,
'We're still struggling with adolescence!'

Acknowledgments

I have many people to thank...

First of all, my amazing children—Jon and Nicole LaFollette—for inspiring the writing of these poems in the first place. And for encouraging me to continue my writing, even though their wisdom and compassion surpass mine... and to my dear daughter-in-law and friend, Eva LaFollette, whose encouragement and interest are so appreciated.

My wonderful stepchildren, Debbie and John Bacon, Jeff and Sandy Ellison, and Tom and Sue Ellison who, with their children and grandchildren, continue to be a major part of my life; and are loved deeply by me. These poems are for you, too.

My good friends who have received a poem or two of mine in their Christmas cards these many years, for complimenting me on the messages in my poems. Your encouragement kept me writing and gave me the courage to publish.

To Kim Kiyosaki who introduced me to the right person to get the publishing process under way... Mona Gambetta with Brisance Books Group. I marvel at her experience and know-how to make these books happen.

To Amy Anderson, Sonya Kopetz, Kerri Kazarba Schneider, and Ingrid Pape-Sheldon, my very creative public relations team of experts, who have carried my story to the world.

And finally, to John B. Laughlin, a fellow traveler in life, who encourages me every day in the writing and publishing process. John, I love having you in my cheering section.

BOOKS OF LOVE
by Kathryn Carole Ellison

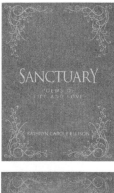